MAKING "MOVIES"
Without a Camera

Other Books by Lafe Locke:

Film Animation Techniques
The Name of the Game
Adventures in Advertising
Exploring Advertising Design
Card Sense and Nonsense

MAKING "MOVIES" Without a Camera

Inexpensive Fun with Flip Books and Other Animation Gadgets

Lafe Locke

BETTERWAY BOOKS
Cincinnati, Ohio

Cover design by Lafe Locke
Illustrations by Lafe Locke
Typography & Prepress Services by Studio 500 Associates

Note: For your convenience, permission is granted to
photocopy the pattern drawings in this book for
your personal use.

97 96 95 94 93 5 4 3 2 1

Library of Congress Cataloging-in-Publication Data

Locke, Lafe.
  Making "movies" without a camera : inexpensive fun with flip books and other
animation gadgets / Lafe Locke.
    p. cm.
  Includes index.
  Summary: Demonstrates how to create animation without a camera and provides
    instructions for making flip books and other animation devices.
  ISBN 1-55870-261-X (paperback) : $7.95
  1. Animation (Cinematography)—Instruments—Juvenile literature. 2. Toy and
    movable books—Specimens. [1. Animation (Cinematography) 2. Toy and
    movable books—Design.] I. Title.
TR897.5.L633 1992
741.5'8—dc20   92-17362
                                                        CIP
                                                         AC

Contents

1.
How Your Eyes Fool You

When you look at an animated cartoon in a movie theater or on your television screen, you are looking at twenty-four different pictures every second. The pictures don't actually move. But they look as if they are moving because each picture is slightly different than the one you see before it. When they are flashed on the screen one after another, they blend together into a moving picture.

PERSISTENCE OF VISION

How come you don't see the change from one picture to the next? It all happens so fast that your eye keeps one image in view for a tiny fraction of a second after it has been removed. By that time you are already looking at the next image.

This is called "persistence of vision," and if you want to prove it to yourself, just shake your hand. Hold your hand about six inches in front of your face with your fingers spread out. Shake your hand rapidly up and down

and you'll think you are seeing eight or ten fingers instead of just a normal handful. It's an optical illusion caused by your persistence of vision — and that's what makes cartoon animation possible.

In this book, there are lots of easy-to-draw pictures you can animate. Some you don't even have to draw, they can be photocopied. You will also be shown how easy it is to put drawings together in various ways to make "movies" of your own, without film, without a camera, without a doubt.

2.

Motion Pictures Your Great-Great-Great-Grandparents Saw

EARLY ANIMATION DEVICES

For about 30,000 years, ever since our relatives were scratching pictures on the walls of caves, man has been thinking about making the pictures move. Finally, in the seventeenth century, the magic lantern was invented for projecting pictures on a wall or a screen. Then, a century later, a Dutch scientist came up with the idea of projecting the pictures in rapid-fire order so that they would appear to move.

From then on, a number of crude animation devices with tongue-twisting names were invented, such as the thaumatrope, phenakistoscope, zoetrope, animatoscope, fantascope, filoscope, praxinoscope, and stroboscope.

The first three named above are easier to make than pronounce, so just for fun let's make them. According to which one you choose — or all of them — you'll need a ruler, scissors, and a single-edge razor blade or X-Acto knife for cutting paper and cardboard. A compass is needed for drawing circles.

A thaumatrope is the easiest to make, so let's start with it.

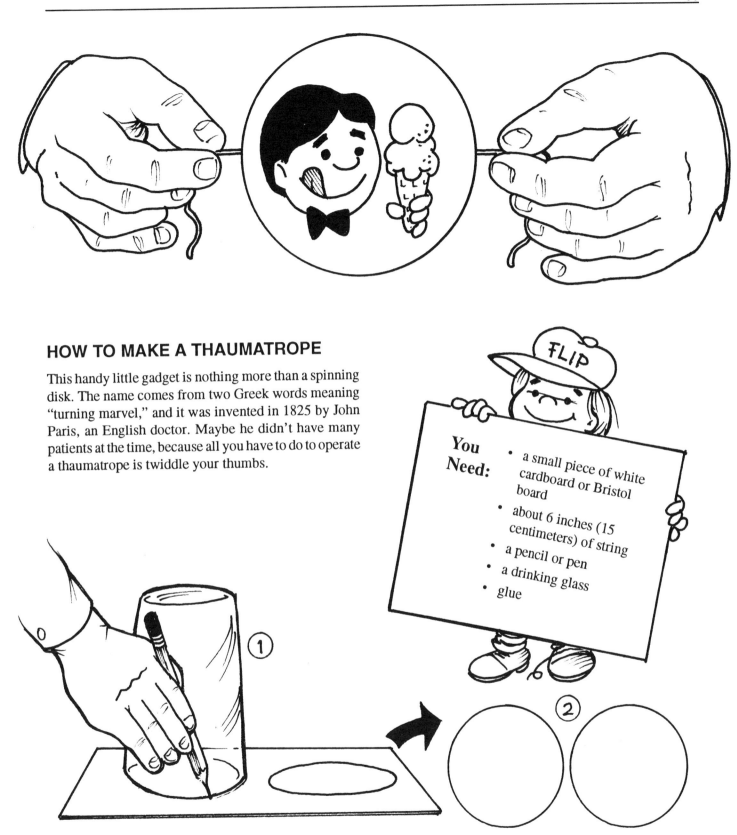

HOW TO MAKE A THAUMATROPE

This handy little gadget is nothing more than a spinning disk. The name comes from two Greek words meaning "turning marvel," and it was invented in 1825 by John Paris, an English doctor. Maybe he didn't have many patients at the time, because all you have to do to operate a thaumatrope is twiddle your thumbs.

You Need:
- a small piece of white cardboard or Bristol board
- about 6 inches (15 centimeters) of string
- a pencil or pen
- a drinking glass
- glue

1. Two-ply Bristol board is best for this because of its whiteness. Cardboard will do if one side of it is white. Turn the drinking glass upside down on the white board and trace around it to make two circles the same size.

2. Cut out the two circles. You now have two white disks.

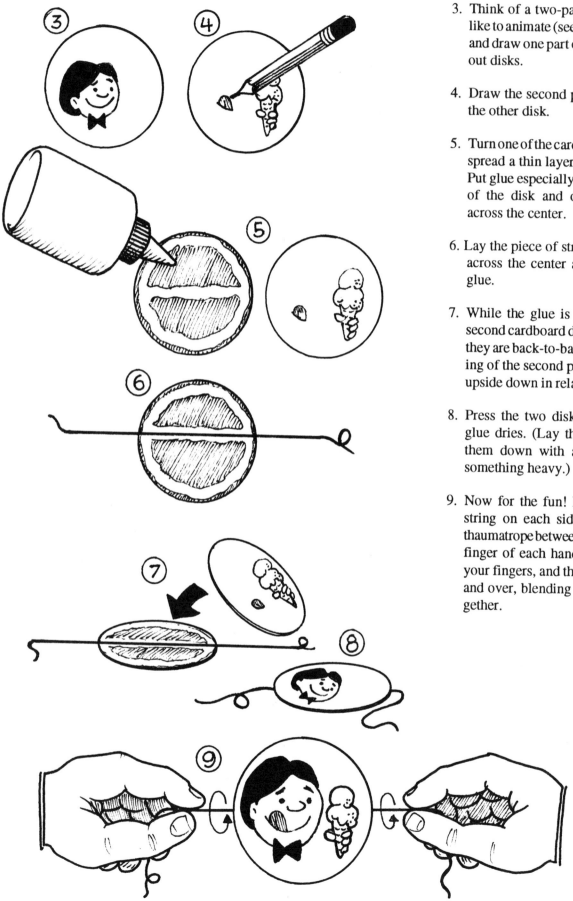

3. Think of a two-part picture you would like to animate (see page 9 for examples) and draw one part of it on one of the cut-out disks.

4. Draw the second part of the picture on the other disk.

5. Turn one of the cardboard disks over and spread a thin layer of glue on the back. Put glue especially around the outer rim of the disk and on a horizontal line across the center.

6. Lay the piece of string in a straight line across the center and press it into the glue.

7. While the glue is still tacky, glue the second cardboard disk to the first so that they are back-to-back. Be sure the drawing of the second part of your picture is upside down in relation to the first part.

8. Press the two disks together until the glue dries. (Lay them flat and weight them down with a book, a brick, or something heavy.)

9. Now for the fun! Hold the lengths of string on each side of the completed thaumatrope between the thumb and forefinger of each hand. Roll the string in your fingers, and the disk will turn over and over, blending the two pictures together.

HOW TO MAKE A PHENAKISTOSCOPE

Joseph Plateau, the Belgian artist-scientist who invented this gadget in 1832, named it after a Greek word meaning "to cheat" because he said it tricks the eye. It employs a series of viewing slots ("shutters") and is said to be the great-granddaddy of the modern movie projector. There are two versions of the phenakistoscope. Plateau's version needs two spinning disks. A simpler form uses only one disk and a mirror. We'll make that one.

You Need:
- white paper at least 8 inches (20 centimeters) square
- black cardboard or Bristol board the same size as the paper
- a pencil or pen
- glue
- a stick about 10 inches (25 centimeters) long and 1/2 inch (1.25 centimeters) thick
- a thumbtack or pushpin

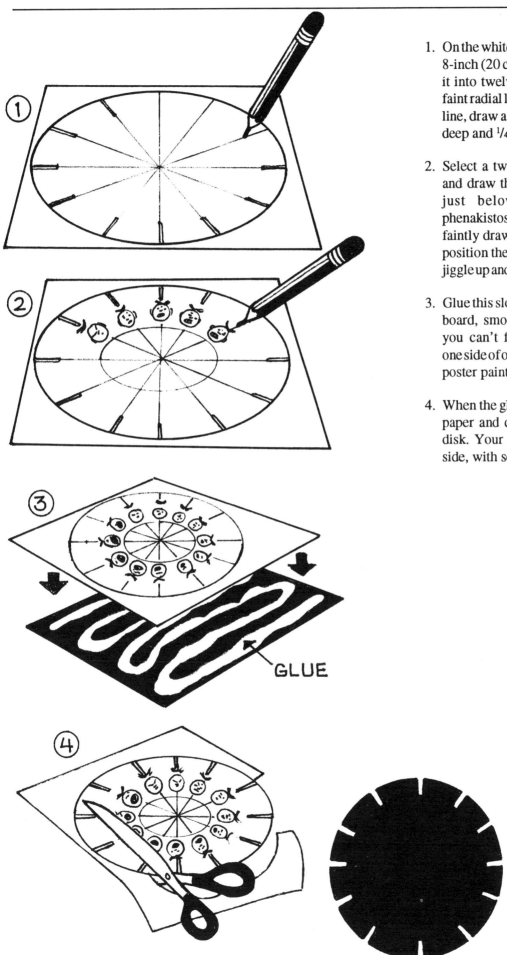

1. On the white paper, draw a circle with an 8-inch (20 centimeter) diameter. Divide it into twelve equal sections with very faint radial lines. At the outer end of each line, draw a slot 1 inch (2.5 centimeters) deep and ¼ inch (.63 centimeter) wide.

2. Select a twelve-part animation subject and draw the images around the circle just below the slots. (See the phenakistoscope disk on page 17.) A faintly drawn inner circle will help you position the images so that they will not jiggle up and down when they are viewed.

3. Glue this slotted circle to the black cardboard, smoothing out all wrinkles. (If you can't find black cardboard, paint one side of ordinary cardboard with black poster paint.)

4. When the glue is dry, cut away the extra paper and cardboard to form a slotted disk. Your drawings should be on one side, with solid black on the other.

GLUE

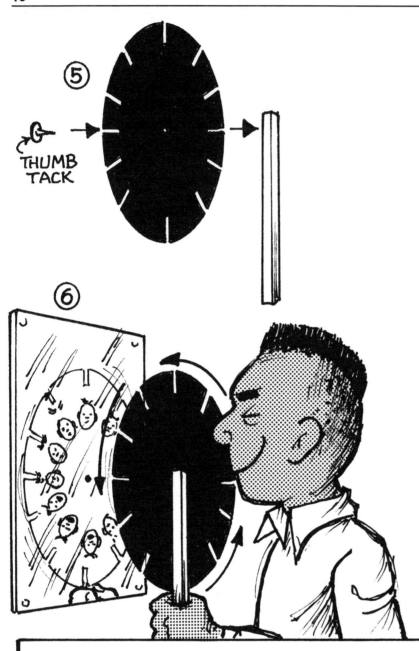

THUMB TACK

5. Push a thumbtack or pushpin through the exact center of the disk and into your wooden stick near one end. The black side of the disk should be next to the stick. The part of the stick extending beyond the disk is your handle for gripping it. (A long pencil can be substituted for the stick. Push the thumbtack into the rubber eraser.) Spin the disk a few times so that it will turn freely on its thumbtack "axle."

6. Now hold up the disk before the mirror with the white, drawn-on side facing the glass. Look through the top slot and spin the disk with your free hand. As the disk turns, your drawn images will merge into a smooth and continuous action. Phenakistic!

Some Helpful Hints

You may trace or photocopy the phenakistoscope disk on the opposite page or on page 119. Glue it to the black cardboard just like in the previous instructions.

If you are uncertain about drawing figures on your first disk, draw them lightly in pencil and see how they move when you spin the disk before the mirror. Make corrections if needed, then trace over the pencil lines with black ink or a felt marking pen.

A lamp that shines light between the disk and the mirror will make your animation easier to see.

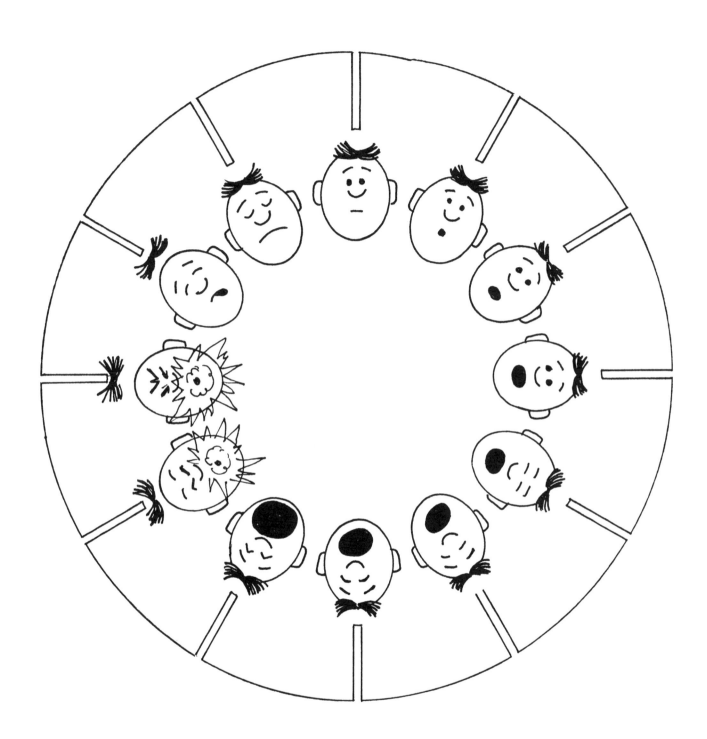

PHOTOCOPY THE SNEEZER ABOVE AND GLUE TO A CARDBOARD DISC.

HOW TO MAKE A ZOETROPE

Back around the turn of the century, nearly every kid on the block had a zoetrope. It was the Nintendo® of the times. The zoetrope was invented in 1834 by a man named William Horner. He gave it the name zoetrope from a Greek word meaning "wheel of life." That's a good description, too, because it's a shallow cylinder with slots around it and a series of pictures on the inside walls. When the cylinder rotates, the pictures come to life.

Perhaps a big reason the zoetrope was such a popular toy was that the animated pictures were on strips of paper. These strips could be interchanged, so any number of capering pictures could be viewed.

You Need:
- a piece of very thick illustration board
- thin plywood (optional)
- flexible Bristol board or thin white cardboard at least 26 inches (65 centimeters) long
- white paper 26 inches (65 centimeters) long
- pencil and pen or black marker
- glue
- black poster paint and brush

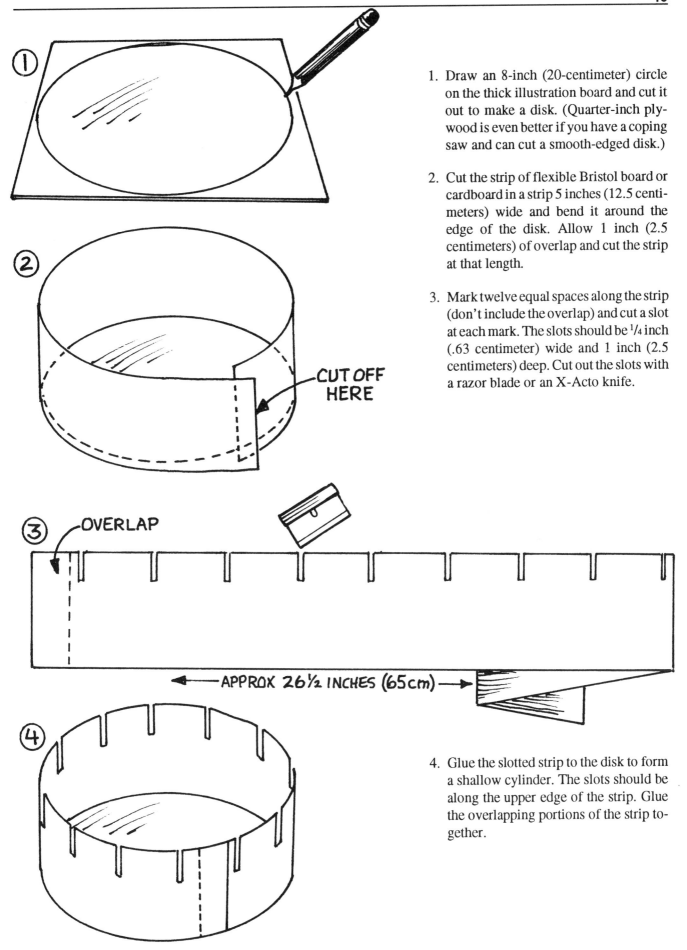

1. Draw an 8-inch (20-centimeter) circle on the thick illustration board and cut it out to make a disk. (Quarter-inch plywood is even better if you have a coping saw and can cut a smooth-edged disk.)

2. Cut the strip of flexible Bristol board or cardboard in a strip 5 inches (12.5 centimeters) wide and bend it around the edge of the disk. Allow 1 inch (2.5 centimeters) of overlap and cut the strip at that length.

3. Mark twelve equal spaces along the strip (don't include the overlap) and cut a slot at each mark. The slots should be 1/4 inch (.63 centimeter) wide and 1 inch (2.5 centimeters) deep. Cut out the slots with a razor blade or an X-Acto knife.

CUT OFF HERE

OVERLAP

APPROX 26½ INCHES (65 cm)

4. Glue the slotted strip to the disk to form a shallow cylinder. The slots should be along the upper edge of the strip. Glue the overlapping portions of the strip together.

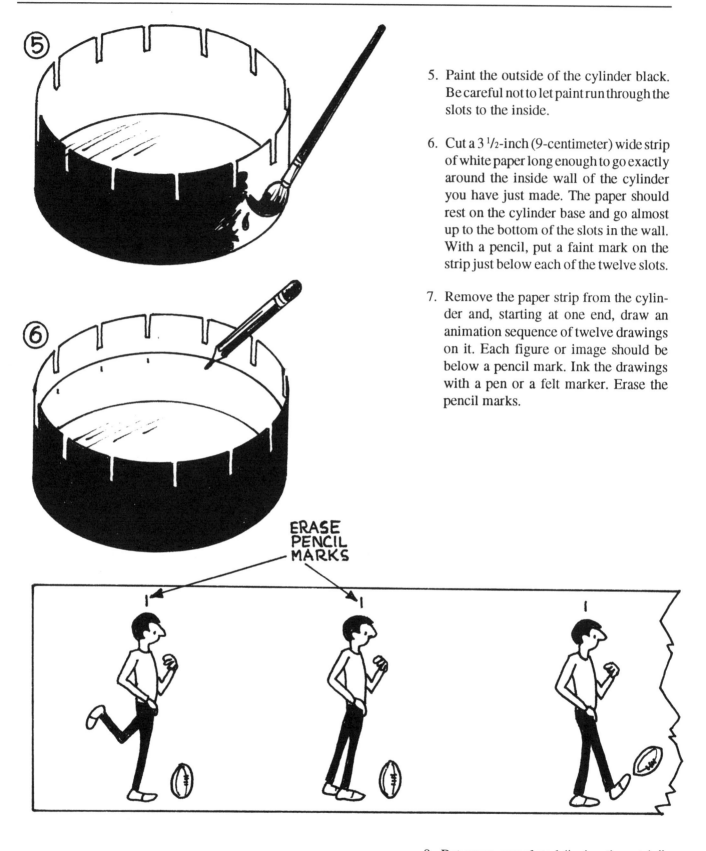

5. Paint the outside of the cylinder black. Be careful not to let paint run through the slots to the inside.

6. Cut a 3 1/2-inch (9-centimeter) wide strip of white paper long enough to go exactly around the inside wall of the cylinder you have just made. The paper should rest on the cylinder base and go almost up to the bottom of the slots in the wall. With a pencil, put a faint mark on the strip just below each of the twelve slots.

7. Remove the paper strip from the cylinder and, starting at one end, draw an animation sequence of twelve drawings on it. Each figure or image should be below a pencil mark. Ink the drawings with a pen or a felt marker. Erase the pencil marks.

ERASE PENCIL MARKS

8. Put your completed "animation strip" back in the cylinder with the drawings directly below the slots. Your zoetrope is ready for viewing, but ... it needs something to turn on.

How to Make It Go

There are three easy ways to mount your zoetrope so that it will revolve:

1. Simply drill a hole in the center of the cylinder base and place it on a record player turntable. Peer through the slots as they pass your eye.

2. Glue a thread spool to a square board. Put a short bolt through the hole in the center of the cylinder and into the hole in the spool. Rotate the cylinder with your hand.

3. Don't drill a hole in the cylinder. Instead, drive a small nail through the center and into one end of a wooden handle. (A short length of broomstick is ideal for a handle. A washer or smooth plastic button on top of the handle will help the cylinder turn.)

Hold the stick in one hand and spin the cylinder with the other as you peer through the passing slots.

WANT A STARTER STRIP FOR YOUR ZOETROPE? YOU CAN PHOTOCOPY OR TRACE THE ONE ON THE NEXT TWO PAGES.

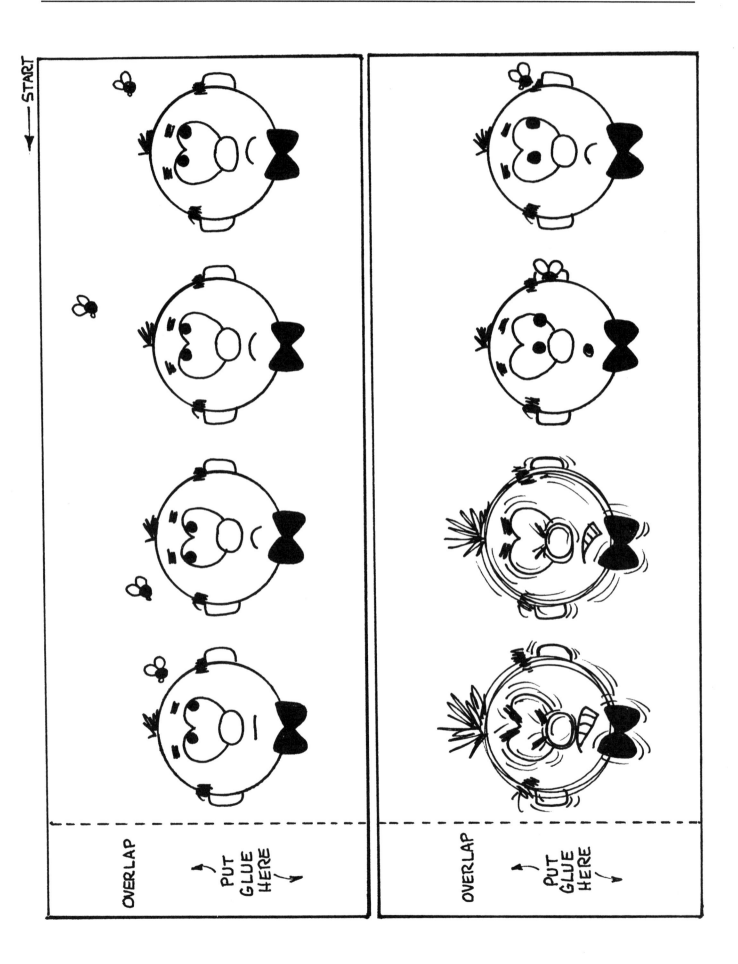

Trace or photocopy the three sections, then cut out and glue them together. Use the same dimensions when drawing your own zoetrope strips.

3.
Flip Books: Movies You Can Put in Your Pocket

MAKING A BOOK

A blank book is nothing more than a small pad of paper with the pages fastened together along one end. Since you hold this pad in one hand and flip the pages with the thumb of your other hand, an ideal size for your flip book is 3 x 5 inches (7.5 x 12.5 centimeters).

You can buy such pads in office supply and stationery stores. They're the little memo pads for carrying in your pocket, and they usually have about fifty pages. If you buy a pad, try to find one that doesn't have blue lines ruled on it. The lines won't be a problem, but pads with plain white paper are best. You can buy small sketch pads with plain paper in art supply stores, but these are more expensive than memo pads.

It's more fun to make your own flip book. You can easily do this, first by figuring the number of pages you will need for your animated action, and then cutting the pages from sheets of typewriter or similar paper. Make them 3 x 5 inches (7.5 x 12.5 centimeters) and cut plenty of extra pages. A total of about fifty is advisable.

Also cut a stiff cardboard backing for your book, the same size as the pages. This will help you to hold it when flipping the pages and will keep the binding from bending.

Before binding the cut-out pages and backing together, make sure all the pages are lined up evenly along the open end.

To bind the flip book pages together, paint rubber cement along one of the short ends, then reinforce this by putting a rubber band around the pages near the bound end. Here are three more ways to strengthen your rubber cement binding:

1. Punch two holes near the bound end and tie the pages together with a string.

2. If there aren't many pages in your flip book, use a heavy-duty office stapler.

3. A strong binder clip will provide temporary reinforcement.

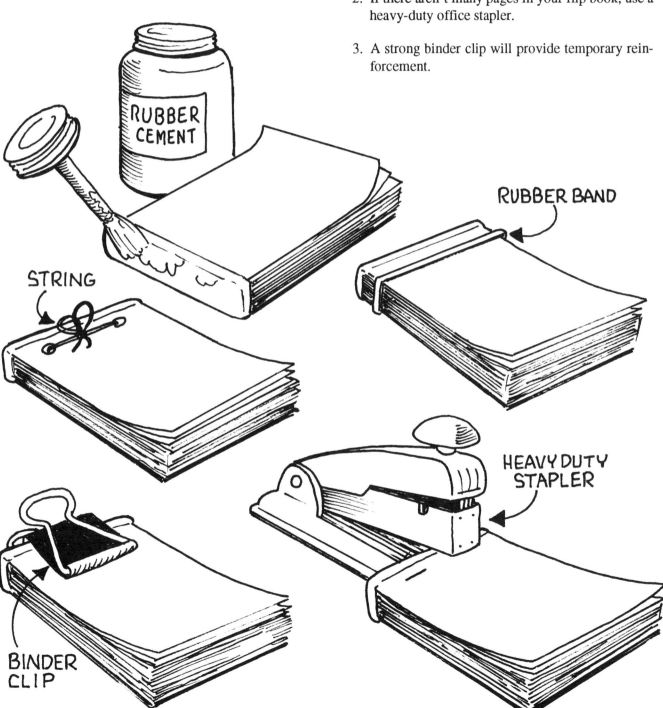

WHAT TO DRAW?

Watch the animated cartoons on television and notice how simply the characters are drawn. There aren't a lot of scratchy lines or fine detail. This is because the characters have to be traced again and again — as many as 1,680 times to make one minute of animation. So, take a hint from the professional animators and keep your flip book drawings uncomplicated, too. Use simple shapes and as few lines as possible.

PREPARING A PATTERN

Once you've decided what you want to show, draw it exactly as it should be in the flip book, but on a separate piece of paper. This will be the pattern that you will copy over and over on the book pages. Draw the pattern in bold black lines with ink or a marker pen so that it will show through each page of the flip book to make tracing possible.

Cut around the pattern, leaving enough margin so you can easily hold it steady under a flip book page while tracing.

TRACING YOUR DRAWINGS

Flip books are riffled (flipped) from back to front, so always work from back to front when drawing in the book. Trace the first drawing on the last page next to the stiff backing, then move toward the front, page by page. Chances are, as you lay down each page on top of the one you have just completed, you'll be able to see the previous drawing through it. This will help you position the next tracing.

The cartoons you see on television move smoothly because they move only a tiny space in each separate frame. To get that same smoothness, you should move the figure in your flip book only $1/8$ inch (.4 centimeter) each time you trace it. That's only about the width of a matchstick. If you get impatient and start spacing out the drawings, your figures will move too fast to be effective.

Place all your drawings on the outer half of the pages — that is, on the half nearest the open end of the flip book — so they may be easily seen. That means you'll draw in a rectangle 3 x 2 $1/2$ inches (7.5 x 6.25 centimeters).

Do your tracings first in pencil. If, when you check them by flipping the pages, they are not all in the right positions, you can erase and correct them. When all are okay, go over the lines with black ink or a fine-pointed felt marker.

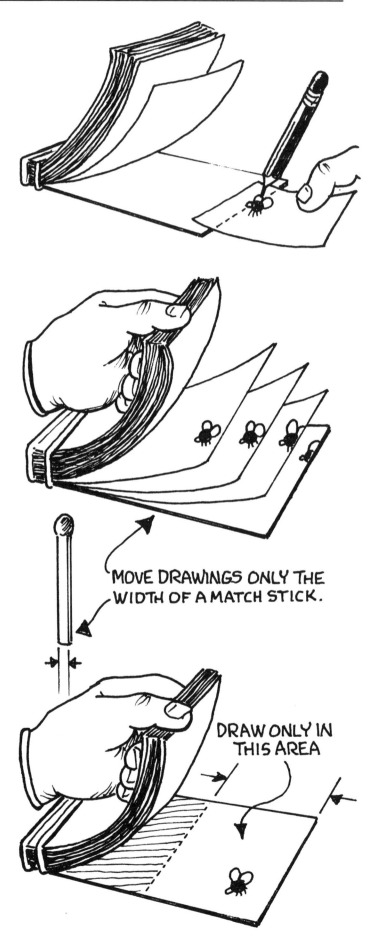

MOVE DRAWINGS ONLY THE WIDTH OF A MATCH STICK.

DRAW ONLY IN THIS AREA

WORKING WITH LOOSE PAGES

You may want to do the tracing on loose pages, then bind your flip book together. First cut a plentiful supply of pages. Next, slide your pattern under a loose page and trace it. Before you trace on the second page, number the first one in the upper left-hand corner. Numbering helps you keep the loose pages in the correct order. The numerals in the upper left-hand corner will be out of sight when the pages are bound together.

When the first page is completed, place the pattern under the second one, moving the pattern about ⅛ inch (.4 centimeter). Use the first page to guide you with positioning. Trace and number the second page, then proceed to others.

Before binding the pages together, remember that they should be arranged with page number one on the bottom of the stack. Grip them firmly in one hand and flip the pages to check the action. If all is in order, bind your flip book by one of the methods shown on page 25.

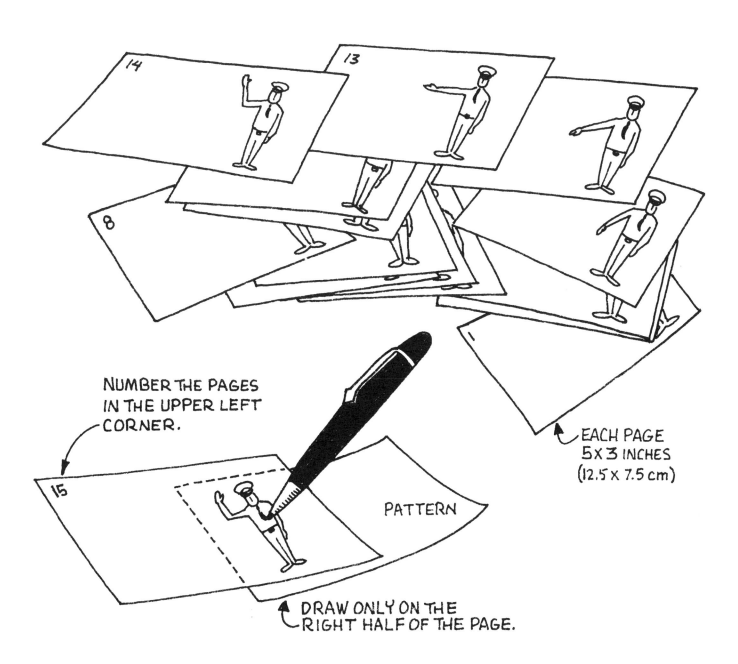

NUMBER THE PAGES IN THE UPPER LEFT CORNER.

EACH PAGE 5 X 3 INCHES (12.5 X 7.5 cm)

PATTERN

DRAW ONLY ON THE RIGHT HALF OF THE PAGE.

HOW TO HOLD AND FLIP THE PAGES

Some like 'em up and down, some like 'em sideways. The drawings on this page show two ways you can grip and flip the pages of your flip book. As you can see, in one case the book is held horizontally, in the other it's held vertically. Before you draw in a blank flip book, decide which way you prefer to hold it. This will determine how you will position your drawings on the pages.

Or perhaps the action you want to draw will determine how you hold the flip book. Does it go better in a horizontal rectangle or a vertical one? Decide before you draw.

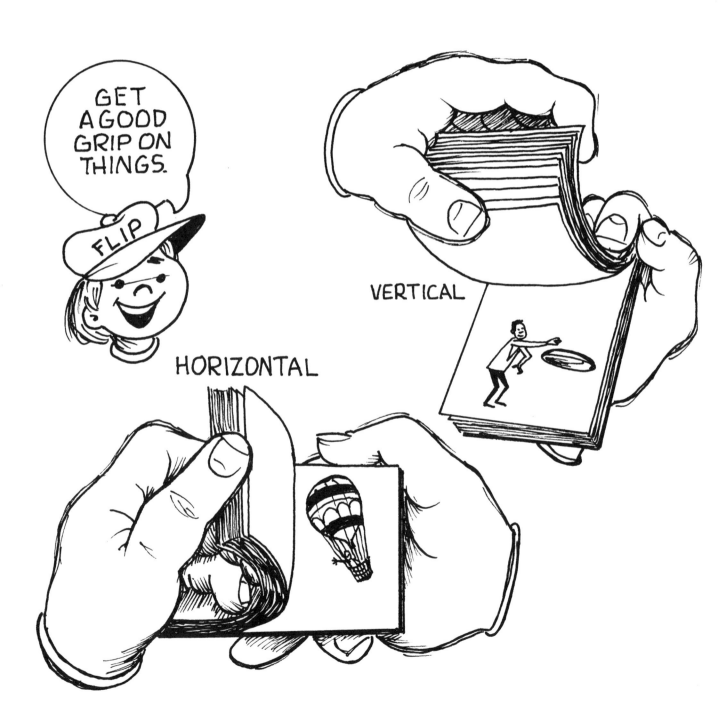

4.
Let's Get Flipping!

TIPS WORTH REPEATING BEFORE YOU START

Got your blank flip book all ready to go? Then read these important tips before you start drawing in it. They will save you time, trouble, and disappointment.

• Decide how you'll hold your flip book — vertically or horizontally — before you begin to draw.

• Keep your drawings simple, with as few lines as possible. You'll be glad you did when you have to trace a drawing dozens of times.

• Make a tracing pattern and provide a margin around it for holding. Use the pattern to keep the drawings uniform, avoiding wibbly-wobbles.

• Start your drawings on the last page and work forward. That's the way you will flip the pages for best results.

• Move each succeeding drawing only ⅛ inch (.4 centimeter) to keep movement from being too rapid.

• Make all drawings in pencil first so they can be erased and corrected if need be.

• Do some flipping every few pages to check the action.

• When all the drawings are penciled in and everything is hunky-dory, trace over the pencil lines with black ink or a fine-pointed felt marker.

REPEATED PATTERNS

The series of drawings across the top of these two pages shows the imaginary flight of a buzzing bee. If you'd like to use this animated series in your first flip book, go to it! You can trace or photocopy the drawing at the right to use as your pattern.

The bees in the frames above are drawn to give a general impression of a busy bee's flight. They are too far apart for effective use in a flip book. When you draw yours, move the bee only a small space at a time as described on page 28. Make it loop-the-loop, zoom, and zigzag. Even though you move it a tiny space on each succeeding page, when you riffle the pages of your flip book, you'll have a lively buzzing bee.

A step-by-step procedure begins below.

TRACE OR PHOTOCOPY THIS PATTERN

1. First prepare your pattern. Draw or copy it and cut it out, leaving plenty of margin for easy handling. Go over the drawing with black ink or a fine-pointed felt marker.

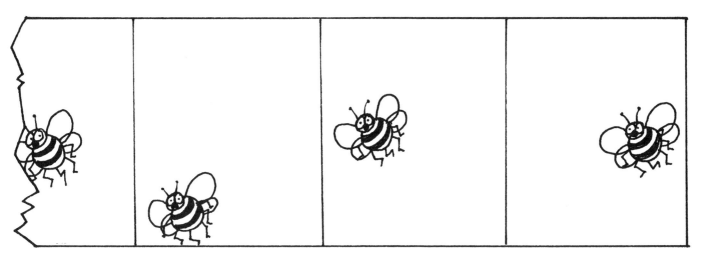

2. Lift all the pages of the flip book and place the bee pattern in the first position on the cardboard backing as if it is just flying in. It doesn't even have to be all the way on the page.

3. Lower the last page of the flip book onto the bee and trace it carefully with a pencil.

4. Remove the pattern from beneath the last page and place it on top of the page. Position the bee 1/8 inch (.4 centimeter) ahead of the one you have just drawn, moving it in the direction you want it to fly. Lower the next page on top of the pattern and trace as before. Repeat this positioning and tracing until you decide the bee can buzz off.

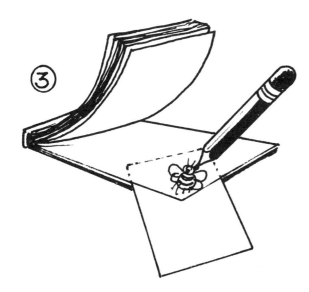

MORE REPEATED PATTERNS

You don't have to trace ALL of a repeated pattern again and again to get interesting animation. Two examples of this are shown below. One makes a flower grow, the other gradually forms a happy face. In each, you start by drawing only a small bit of the pattern, then add a bit more on each page.

If you use these patterns, keep the action going. Add more flowers to the pot. Darken the man's hair, add glasses, a mustache, maybe even a beard.

In the bottom strip, the whole pattern is repeated as it is moved only a small space at a time. Note that the little plane hits an air pocket and bounces up and down.

NOW YOU SEE IT, NOW YOU DON'T

Some actions are hard to squeeze onto a half-page in a flip book. So put on a disappearing act and let your imagination supply some of the movement. In other words, let the action go right off the page, then return, going in the opposite direction. Thus the racing car below, or anything else you want, can zigzag across your flip book pages as many times as you want.

Imagine that the racing car below is on a figure-eight track. Here is how to handle the action:

1. Trace the pattern below in ink or with a black marker on tracing paper or paper thin enough that you can see the drawing though it when the pattern is turned over.

2. Position your pattern under the left side of the last page of your flip book with the pattern barely showing. Trace it.

3. Remove the pattern and reinsert it under the next page so that the racing car has moved, angling down to the right by 1/8 inch (.4 centimeter). Trace it again. Follow this procedure until the racer has moved off the page at the lower right corner.

4. Leave five or six flip book pages blank. (Imagine the racer is out of sight and looping back.)

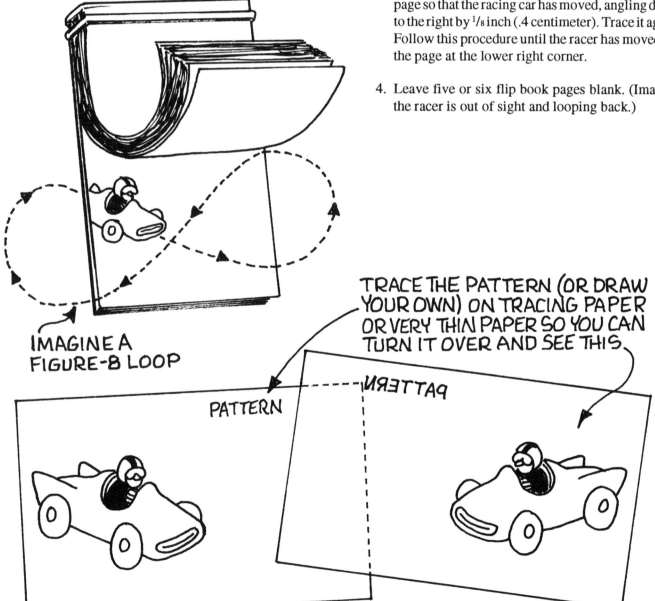

IMAGINE A FIGURE-8 LOOP

TRACE THE PATTERN (OR DRAW YOUR OWN) ON TRACING PAPER OR VERY THIN PAPER SO YOU CAN TURN IT OVER AND SEE THIS

PATTERN

PATTERN

5. Turn the pattern over so that the racer faces to the left. Position it at the upper right-hand corner of the next flip book page and start the series of tracings that will take it out of sight at the lower left.

6. You can repeat the cycle as many times as the pages in your flip book permit.

This is a great gimmick for actions that seem to cover a lot of distance right and left or up and down. For example, a jogger, skier, flying carpet, soaring bird, and hopping kangaroo. The airplane on page 35 can be treated this way, as well as other examples in this book. You can even break the rule about drawing only on the outer half of the page and use the hidden area near the binding to your advantage. If you traced the sequence below in a vertical flip book (see opposite page), the balloon would go out of sight into the hidden area and the parachutist would come down out of it. For this action, you will need two separate patterns.

MOVE THE BALLOON IN AT THE BOTTOM AND OUT AT THE TOP.

MOVE THE CHUTE IN AT THE TOP AND OUT AT THE BOTTOM.

PATTERN #1

PATTERN #2

STILL MORE REPEATED PATTERNS

The drawings in the sequences below have been moved more than the recommended ¹/₈ inch (.4 centimeter). If you copy them, insert the missing in-between drawings.

For example, show just the tip of the flying carpet entering on the left, then make about fourteen or fifteen drawings to get it out of sight off the right-hand side of

the page. Turn the pattern over (as was described on page 36) and trace the little flyer coming back in the opposite direction. You could even make him loop-the-loop like the skateboarder.

There actually are three patterns for the bottom sequence. The hen and the egg are used again and again, but the hand is popped on at the very last.

CHANGING PATTERNS

Not all flip books have repeated patterns, of course. In fact, the most exciting ones have drawings that change from page to page. If you've worked your way through the previous pages of this book, now is the time to graduate to projects with changing patterns. They're a bit more difficult, but a lot more fun in the end.

Obviously, a flip book with changing patterns requires more preparation than one with repeated patterns. Each drawing is different from the one preceding it, yet each drawing must be to the same scale and have certain similarities to the one that went before. For example, if you show a dancing girl, you'll want her to look the same in every movement — not a fat girl in one picture and a bean pole in another.

To achieve a constant likeness, it's best to:

• Establish a "key drawing" at the start. That's film animators' talk for a drawing that establishes what the girl looks like and what she's wearing. Use your key drawing as a guide in every action the girl takes.

• Draw all your pattern drawings in succession, tracing as much of the key drawing as possible and changing only that portion that moves.

• Number each pattern so you'll be sure to get them in the right order when traced in the flip book.

• Do all of the patterns in pencil first, so you can erase and correct any errors or lines that have gone astray. Then, go over the pencil lines with black ink or a sharp felt marker.

• Now is a good time to double-check the action. Grip the patterns in one hand and flip the pages to see if the action goes as you planned it.

• Finally, trace the patterns into your flip book with ink or a black marker. Though you have drawn the section from start to finish, remember that the individual drawings must go into the flip book pages from back to front.

SOME TIPS FROM FILM ANIMATORS

Here's one you'll get a kick out of. It includes some tricks professional film animators use. For instance:

Limited Animation

Note that, except for six of the drawings, the body and head of the soccer player are the same in each frame. Only a leg and the arms are changed. This trick of changing only a part of a drawing makes it easier and faster to do the drawings. It is borrowed from a practice professional animators call "limited animation." For another example of limited animation, look at the sketches of loose flip book pages on page 29. Only one arm of the saluting soldier moves. The rest of his body stays the same.

You can trace or photocopy these. They are drawn to a size that fits well in a 3 x 5 inch (7.5 x 12.5 centimeter) vertical flip book with plenty of margin. When the soccer ball is booted upward, make it disappear into the binding of the book.

Animation Cycle

Drawings #1 and #18 are identical. The little guy begins by holding the ball in his hands and ends in the same pose. Animators call this a "cycle." Since the action comes back to where it started, you can repeat the cycle again and again to double or triple the length of your flip book show.

Double Framing

Another way to fill up your flip book (always try for thirty or more pages) is to trace each pattern "on twos."

This is an animators' term, also called "double framing" because the same picture appears in two joining frames on the reel of film. Thus, when you trace each pattern below into your flip book, trace it again exactly the same on the following page. Trace the next pattern twice, and the next. When the pages are flipped, your eye's persistence of vision will blend them all together into a smooth-flowing action. This is especially important in Patterns Nine through Thirteen, where the body positions change.

CHANGING PATTERNS: LIMITED ANIMATION

Here are more actions for which you make a key drawing as the basic pattern, then change only a portion of the drawing when you trace the pattern in a flip book.

For example, the firecracker is repeated each time.

All you do is shorten the burning fuse and add some sputter and smoke. Be creative, especially with the big bang at the end. Only the legs of the walking man change from drawing to drawing — until the climax. (Like Flip

says: "Outta sight!") The flying bird's beak and wing are the only changes in the lower sequence. You can make him fly out of the page, then back in again by turning the pattern over, as was explained earlier.

Remember to make several in-between drawings to fill and lengthen these sequences.

MORE LIMITED ANIMATION

In the two actions below, the ostrich with its head in the sand and the fortune cookie are your key drawings.

How does an ostrich know when it's safe to pull its head out of the sand? By coming up for a peek, of course. In your flip book, have him hide his head and take a peek as many times as you like. Try tracing this series "on twos," as was explained on page 42.

The fortune cookie sequence should also be drawn in your flip book "on twos" to provide ample time to read the message as it emerges. This one looks simple,

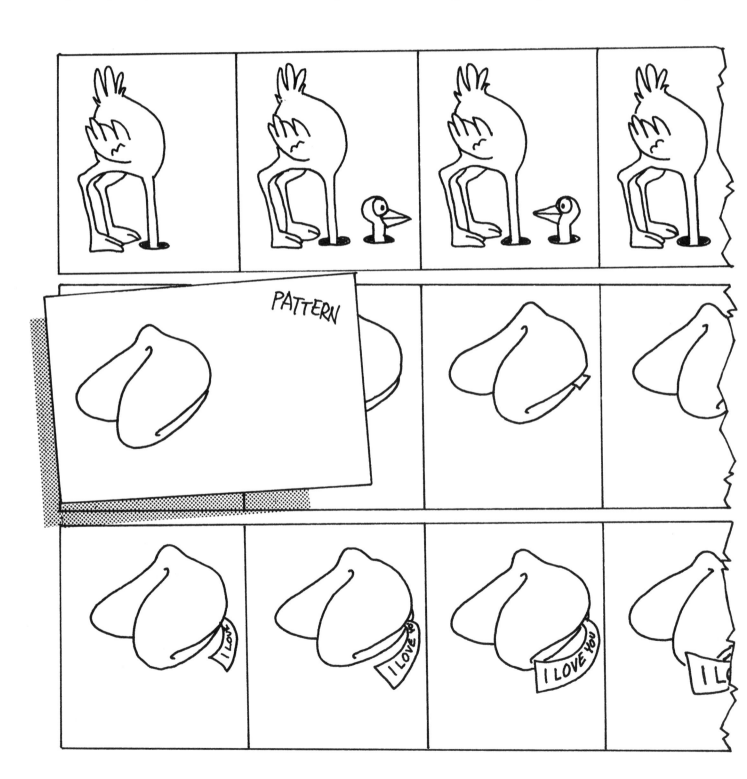

because the drawing is simple — a fortune cookie and a strip of paper. But you may find it difficult to keep the message from being blurred or wibbly-wobbly as it emerges from the cookie and enlarges. In that case, let the slip of paper come out blank, then pop on I LOVE YOU on the last page. Hold it as long as you want to let the message sink in.

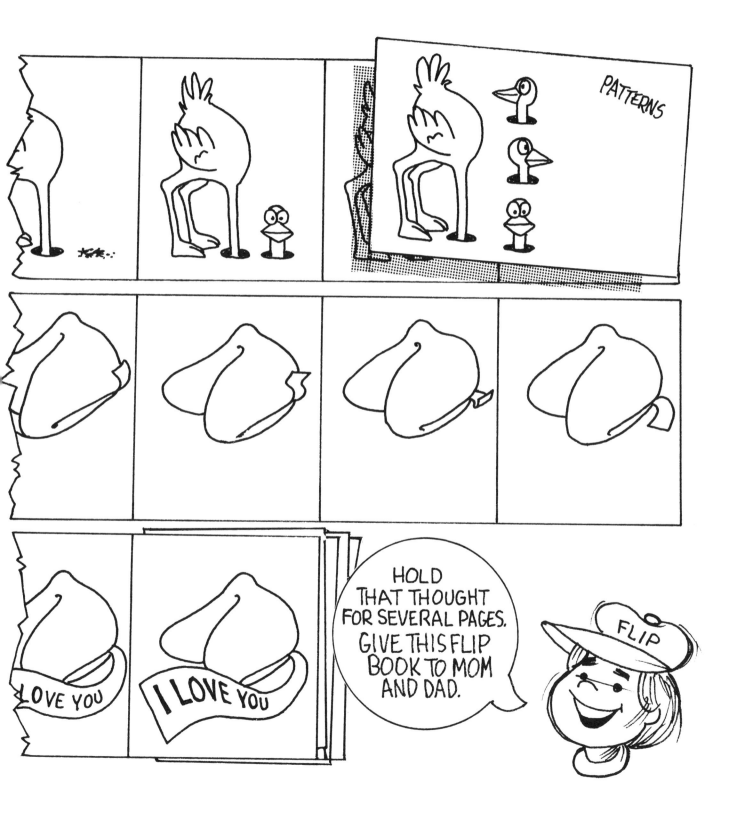

A BLEND OF LIMITED AND FULL ANIMATION

That pesky fly we saw on pages 27 and 28 is back. This time it's pestering a dog, which, after one failed attempt, figures a way to settle the fly's hash.

You can trace the entire sequence shown on these two pages and have a brief episode in a flip book. But if you trace each frame twice, "on twos" that is, you'll have even better action.

As you work with this dog-and-fly episode, study the changes in the dog's expression. They help explain what is going on. In your future flip books, try to use facial expressions — on animals and people — to make your little hand-held visual shows more effective.

FULL ANIMATION

Full animation will make your flip books more interesting and exciting. But you'll have to work harder. When everything moves on every succeeding page, there are more patterns to draw. Then each one has to be traced onto a flip book page.

The eleven patterns shown on these two pages will eliminate some of the work for at least one flip book showing a very happy fellow. These patterns are drawn full-size for use on one-half of a 3 x 5 inch (7.5 x 12.5 centimeter) flip book page. Trace or photocopy them, then trace them in your book "on twos." The patterns are

numbered, but you don't have to use them in any particular order. Use your imagination. How would you hop, skip, and jump about if you felt as happy as this fellow?

You had best try these on loose pages first—until you get the hopping, skipping routine worked out. You may even want to add some patterns of your own. In fact, wouldn't you like to dream up some full animation actions and do all the drawing yourself?

MORE FULL ANIMATION

Here's an action with two bouncy figures showing once again that part of the action can take place completely off the page (see pages 36 and 37). The viewer's imagination supplies what is missing.

Copy these drawings; they're the right size for use in a horizontal 3 x 5 inch (7.5 x 12.5 centimeter) book. But — and here's the rub — you must do two things to make this action better:

1. Draw some "in-betweens." When a figure is rising or coming down, move it only ⅛ of an inch (.4 centimeter) each time you trace it.

2. When the fellow on the right is out of sight and the one on the left is standing and waiting for him to come down, trace that same drawing on four or more pages of the flip book. The pause in the action will make it appear that the parachutist went very, very high in the air.

With the short movements and the brief pause, you'll have an extra long and interesting episode. Be sure there are enough pages in your flip book.

INSERTING IN-BETWEENS

These exercises will help you fine-tune your thinking as well as your drawing skills. Two series of drawings are shown. Both of them can be lengthened and made more interesting by the insertion of new drawings in between the present ones. That's what professional animators call the extra drawings — "in-betweens."

For example, take the girl with a problem. (She's trying to decide what to have for dessert.) Fill in the series with additional drawings showing more facial expressions she might have while racking her brain. This is another instance in which facial expressions are part of the action. (See the dog on pages 48 and 49.)

Try this, too. At the very end, add another thought balloon showing the dessert she decided upon.

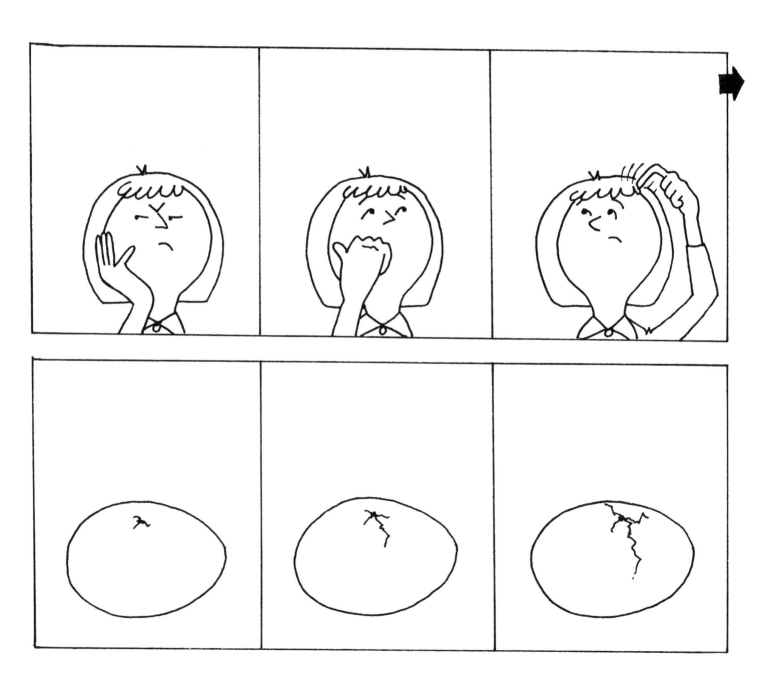

In the egg-hatching scene, your task is to make additional in-between drawings of the egg, enlarging the crack in the shell and making the shell slowly open. At the end, do extra drawings showing the chick flapping his (or her?) wings. Since the action is slow, this is a good series to trace "on twos." Or you can even triple-frame it, tracing each drawing on three consecutive pages in your flip book.

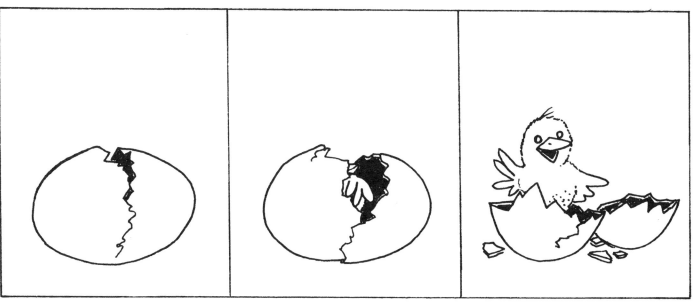

FREEHAND EXERCISES

True to the old saying, the early bird below gets the worm. But it also gets more than it bargained for when the worm turns.

This sequence can be stretched out to some length simply by adding more and more worm turns to thoroughly wrap up the unlucky bird. And since a wiggly worm is hardly something you can trace from a pattern, you can sharpen your skill by drawing this sequence freehand. Use the nine drawings on this and the opposite page simply as guides. Be careful to keep all of your drawings the same relative size, but a little wiggling about won't hurt. It might even add to the fun.

7

8

9

A Clean Sweep

It will probably be easiest to do this one on loose pages and bind them into a flip book when all the drawings are completed.

1. Do four pages of solid black.

2. Start the snail's slow entry at the upper left-hand corner of a page.

3. As you draw the snail's movement across, around, and back and forth on the page, leave a trail of clear white paper behind it.

4. When the entire area has been wiped clean, move the snail slowly off the page.

Remember to reverse the order of the pages when you bind them together so your snail will move forward as the pages are flipped back to front.

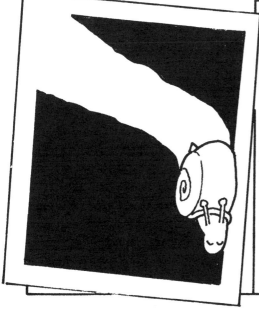

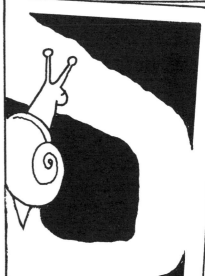

5.
Adding Some Pizazz

Already in this book you have been using some tricks of the professional animator's trade — like in-betweening and drawing on twos. Now, try a whole bag of additional tricks designed to fool the eye and make your drawings more exciting. These devices have names like *cut, pop-on, zoom, wipe, squash*, and *stretch*. They were invented for use in film animation, but you'll find that they are handy in flip books, too.

POP-ONS

When something *suddenly* appears in an established picture, that's a pop-on; like the light bulb, at right, when the girl suddenly gets an idea. The bulb doesn't come on gradually, it appears suddenly — it *pops on*.

The Santa Claus drawings below show how pop-ons can be used in a flip book sequence. The main drawing stays the same, but each speech balloon contains a different picture to show what the greedy kid wants for Christmas. In one drawing, we suddenly see a close-up of Santa and the kid. This is called a *cut*, and there's more about cuts on pages 62 and 63.

MORE POP-ONS

Here are lots of suggestions for pop-ons you can use in flip books. For example, the magician making a bouquet of flowers appear from nowhere, and an arrow suddenly hitting a target. These are just suggestions to set your gray cells working. You'll have to devise a whole series of drawings to make each suggestion into a series of pictures for your flip book. Don't stop there. Think of other pop-ons you can use.

CUTS

Every time you watch a movie, a television show, or even a TV commercial, you see "cuts." That's when the scene suddenly shifts from one view to another, say from a full-length view to a close-up, or to an entirely different scene; from a picture of a dog food can to a shot of a pooch happily gobbling dinner.

Cuts, a standard technique in films and TV, can be used in flip books, too. You have already seen one being used in the Santa Claus drawings on page 59. But remember that flip book action seldom takes more than fifty pictures. One or two cuts should be the limit.

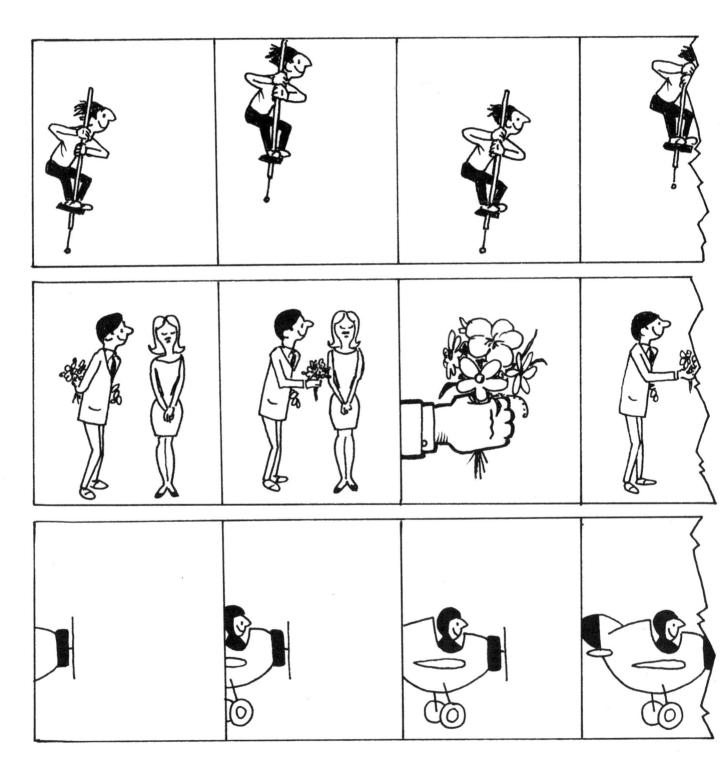

In the examples of cuts shown below, only one drawing is shown for each change of scene. In your flip book, you must repeat each drawing four to six times for it to register in the viewer's eye and mind.

MORE CUTS

Not so fast! Look back at the previous two pages. They show examples of cuts that are from full-length views, called "long shots," to close-ups, then back to long shots. Now, below and on the opposite page, you see cuts to entirely different scenes. They're there to help explain what is going on. Note that the cuts can be the same size as the views that precede them, as in the case of the walking man and the bird and nest. Or you can cut to a

close-up like the kid plugging his ears. In this case, you could even cut to a long view, showing him standing with the firecracker at his feet.

WIPES

Imagine you are in a theater to see a play. The curtain rises and an actress is on stage. First you see her feet, then her legs appear as the curtain goes higher, then her body, shoulders, and head. If you saw the same scene on a movie or television screen, it would look something like the line of drawings immediately below. It would be called a wipe, because the actress is "wiped" into view from a blank screen. (When the curtain goes down, she is wiped off.)

Below there are two other examples of this interesting technique to show that wipes can be done in various shapes and in any direction.

Watch several television programs and see how many wipes you can spot. Practice using them to make your flip book sequences more interesting.

MORE WIPES

The diagrams at the far right show only a very few of the many standard wipes used in films. All can be adapted for flip books. In films, one picture usually wipes off to reveal another beneath it. But this is hard to do in small flip book drawings. So, use simple white or black wipes to reveal the pictures you want to show.

The kite flyer sequence below shows an interesting feature of wipes. Their shape often sets the stage for the scene or action that follows — like a heart-shaped wipe introducing a Valentine message.

The spreading ink blot proves you don't have to use straight lines in wipes. This sequence provides a double-helping of fun, because, if you flip it from front to back instead of back to front, the solid black "ink stained" page will be wiped clean and the ink bottle will right itself.

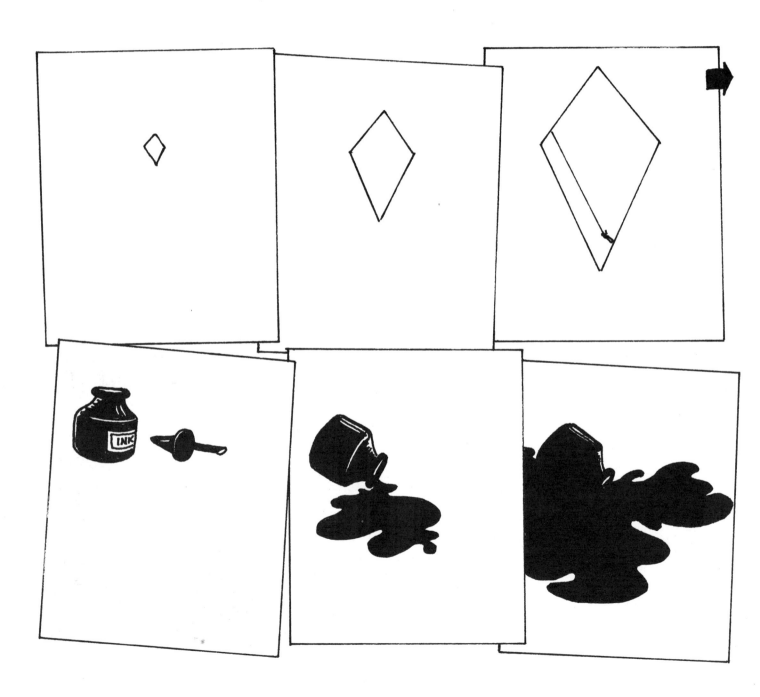

ZOOMS

Zooms are exciting, and they'll add a lively touch to your flip book art. A zoom is a technique borrowed from films in which you draw a figure larger on each successive page (like the lady with the umbrella on the opposite page). Since the viewer's focus moves in closer, this is called zooming in. But you can zoom both in and out. The focus is zooming out in the bottom drawings. If you kept backing off in additional drawings, the kid would be shown in full-length, the balloon bobbing above him.

Zooms, like cuts, are often used to focus attention on an object or a face of special interest. They require more drawings than a cut, but result in smoother action. You can also zoom in and out to create wipes. The boy and the balloon below could start with a completely blank page. Then, by zooming out from the balloon, you wipe on the whole scene. Zoom in to extremely close focus on the ball Flip is holding (far right), and you would eliminate all the drawing, thus wiping the page clean.

STRETCH, SQUASH, DRAG, SWISH

Here are some exercises in exaggeration. Objects are pulled out of shape to show movement and sudden stops. You see this often in animated cartoons, so why not try it in your flip books? A snail is stretched far out of shape as it tries to break the snail speed record, and winds up squashed against a wall in its haste.

A truck in motion is dragged backward by the pull of inertia, then leans forward when it comes to a stop.

Trucks don't really do that, but it's fun to exaggerate in your drawings.

The grasshopper shown here is fastest of all. That's why its body is blurred and shown simply as speed lines. In animators' language, this is called a swish. If you show a swish like this in a flip book, don't draw it "on twos." You'll want the figure to move across the page *fast*.

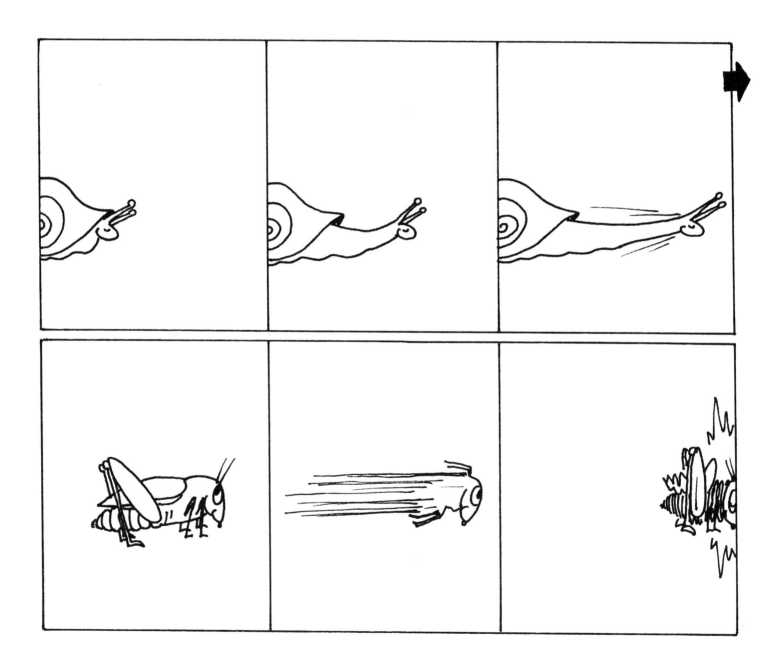

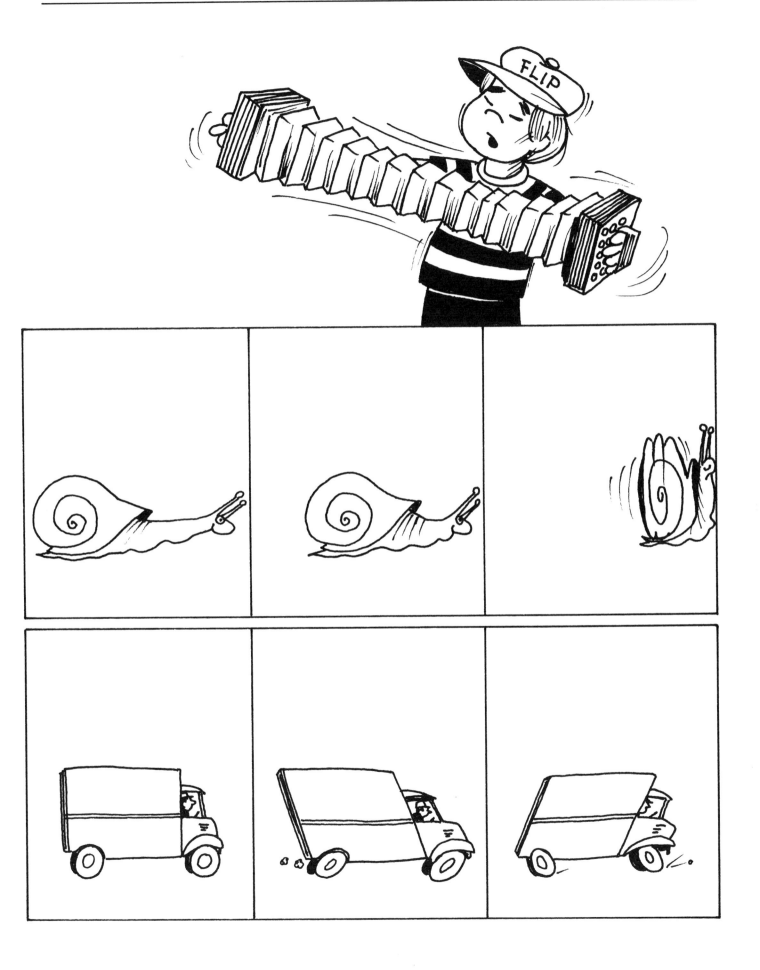

WIGGLE, FLICKER, VIBRATE

One of the problems when drawing flip books is in making identical drawings on each succeeding page so they won't be wiggly and blurred. It takes careful positioning and tracing of each drawing.

On the other hand, there are times when you'll actually *want* your drawings to wiggle to show that they are alive and vibrating. This is easy to accomplish, and some examples are shown below. When drawing a campfire, for instance, vary the flames from page to page (see dotted lines in drawing below), and they'll wave and flicker as the pages are flipped. This same trick can be used when showing waving banners, wavering smoke, expanding balloons, croaking frogs, heavy breathing, and a whole lot more.

COLOR, TOO

Got your felt markers handy? Watercolor or colored inks and pencils will also do. Some drawings just cry out for color — like Santa Claus, traffic lights, red birds, and clown noses.

If you are considering these things — or anything — in a flip book, consider adding color to it to make a really smashing show. Be sure you're using good quality paper so that the colors won't run or bleed through the page. But since you've selected paper with a good snap to it for better flipping, chances are it will take the color very well.

BACKGROUNDS, FOREGROUNDS

Most flip books show a simple action against a blank background. A main reason for this is to keep the drawing to a bare minimum, just enough to get the idea across. But sometimes an added background or foreground will help tell your story better — in fact, it might be needed to explain what's happening. So if you're game, try adding a background or foreground setting to your flip book sequences and see how much better the results are.

If your story, for example, involves a drive in the country, it will need something like the sample background shown immediately below. Note that the background fence and hills are repeated on each page and the little car moves from one side to the other.

On the other hand, in the three top drawings on the opposite page, the little "Sherlock Holmes" remains in the same place and the trail he is following moves from

right to left. This "traveling foreground" is seen often in animated cartoons and, though he is stationary, will give the impression that it is indeed Sherlock who is moving along. Of course, to make the impression believable, you'll have to redraw his legs each time to make him "walk."

Another commonly seen example is that of a stationary figure shown against a moving background. The witch drawing is repeated on every page in the drawing below, and the moon moves across the night sky to make her "fly." You can use a felt marker or gray ink to make the sky.

6.
It's a Gift!

How many times have you bought or even *made* a greeting card for a friend or family member? Here's a great idea for the next time the occasion arises. Show that certain person he or she is something special in your heart by giving a flip book instead of an ordinary card.

Make a special book for Christmas, Easter, a birthday, or any occasion. Add a lot of color to it. Then wrap it like a gift and mail it or deliver it in person. Your unusual gift will be kept and enjoyed long after a greeting card is set aside.

GIVE IT A COVER

If you plan to use your flip books as gifts or special occasion greetings, you should provide them with attractive covers. After all, they are books, aren't they? The cover ought to be drawn or painted in color, especially if the pages of the books are illustrated in black and white. If you use heavier paper for covers, make sure it can be folded back near the edge where the book is bound so the stiffness will not interfere with the flipping of the book's pages.

PSST! Even if you don't plan to use your flip books as gifts or greetings, provide them with attractive covers anyway.

CHRISTMAS GREETINGS

Here are three ideas that can be animated in flip books for special Christmas cheer. They aren't meant to give you a full sequence of action; they're just suggestions to set your mental gears and pencils in motion. Notice that they use a couple animation tricks you've already tried. The tree in the top row of drawings demonstrates an "add-on" method (see page 34), in which you start with just a small portion of a drawing and add a bit more on each following page or two.

The three Santa drawings suggest what can be done with drawings that grow ever-larger on each page. (If these cuts were shot with a camera on film, you'd be zooming in on the old boy.)

If you copy the snoozing shepherd and his sheep, don't worry if you can't trace the lines exactly. Inexact tracings will make them seem to be in motion when they are flipped ... and whoever saw snores and a flock of sheep stand still?

Reminder: In each example, the last page has lettering on it. In your flip book, repeat this page several times so the viewer has time to see clearly and understand the greeting.

HAPPY NEW YEAR

Try these happy ways of greeting the new year, and give them to those you love. Expand the three suggestions into full-length flip books. Print or write any greeting you want on the cover or the final pages ... or both. Add some color!

There are other symbols of the new year season in the sketches at the right. Develop them into additional flip books.

HAPPY BIRTHDAY

Glance over the birthday greeting suggestions on these two pages and you'll see several animation tricks that were discussed earlier — the flickering flame and the vibrating cracker below, for example. The happy little fellow opposite is drawn in full animation, and the fortune cookie can be done with a combination of limited and full animation. The idea of cutting a birthday cake, lower right, is borrowed from the chap with the flowers on page 62.

Note how the fortune cookie, which was used to say "I love you" on page 47, can be used for almost any sort of greetings you want to send.

Remember, you can also print your greetings on the covers of your flip books or on the last few pages.

GET WELL

They say laughter is the best medicine. So, make your "get well" flip books as funny as you can. Funny animals are always welcome, but just about anything that will bring a smile to a sick friend's face is fair game.

Note that any action sequence worked up from the doctor suggestion on the opposite page will require full animation — a series of changing drawings. The rocking cat, on the other hand, can be drawn by titling and tracing the same pattern for most of the pages.

You can zoom in and out on the rabbit and balloon. Do the same thing with the happy face.

CONGRATULATIONS

Graduations, success in reaching any sort of goal, winning contests, engagements, births ... there are dozens of reasons for congratulating your family, friends, and acquaintances. Instead of the usual card, send them a lively flip book to appreciate and enjoy for a long time to come.

The graduate below, for example, can toss his cap right off the page of the flip book. The climbing chart will demonstrate the success of a fund-raising campaign or business. The First Place ribbon is pulled from a hat as if by magic. You take 'em from there.

Like many of these suggestions, your message is saved for the flip book cover or the final few pages because it is difficult to hand-letter a message throughout a flip book and keep the words from blurring.

THINKING OF YOU/THANK YOU

There's that thinking girl again. She offered a lesson in in-betweening (pages 54-55). Now she's demonstrating how you can put her to practical use ... telling your friends you're thinking of them.

The bird and the elephant, or anything else you dream up, can be useful for flip book greetings, too. Notice how the circular wipe you learned on pages 66-67 becomes a double wipe with the pachyderm.

The big-billed bird needs lots of in-betweens as he opens wide to deliver your message.

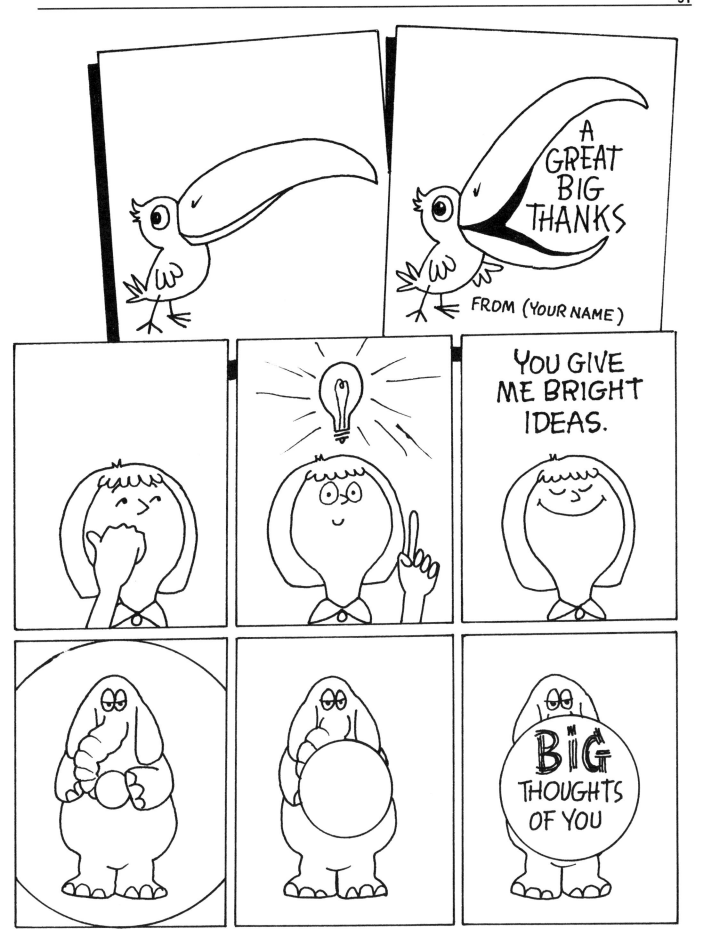

7.
A Flip Book Bonus

IT'S COMPLETE AND READY TO COPY OR CUT OUT.

Up to now, you've been doing most of the work. So, here's a treat — a bonus flip book all ready for you. It starts on the opposite page and all you have to do is cut out the thirty-five numbered pages, bind them together, and start flipping. Flip's pet seal, Flipper, will put on his act.

If you'd rather not cut up the final pages of this book, trace or photocopy the bonus flip book.

Note that this is a *vertical* flip book. It should be bound along the top edge and held as shown in the drawing on page 30. When you gather the cut-out pages for binding, remember to start with the first page on the bottom.

You Need:	• scissors
	• glue
	• a rubber band or heavy staples

I'M THE STAR.

CUT OUT EACH
3X5-INCH
(7.5 X 12.5 cm)
PAGE

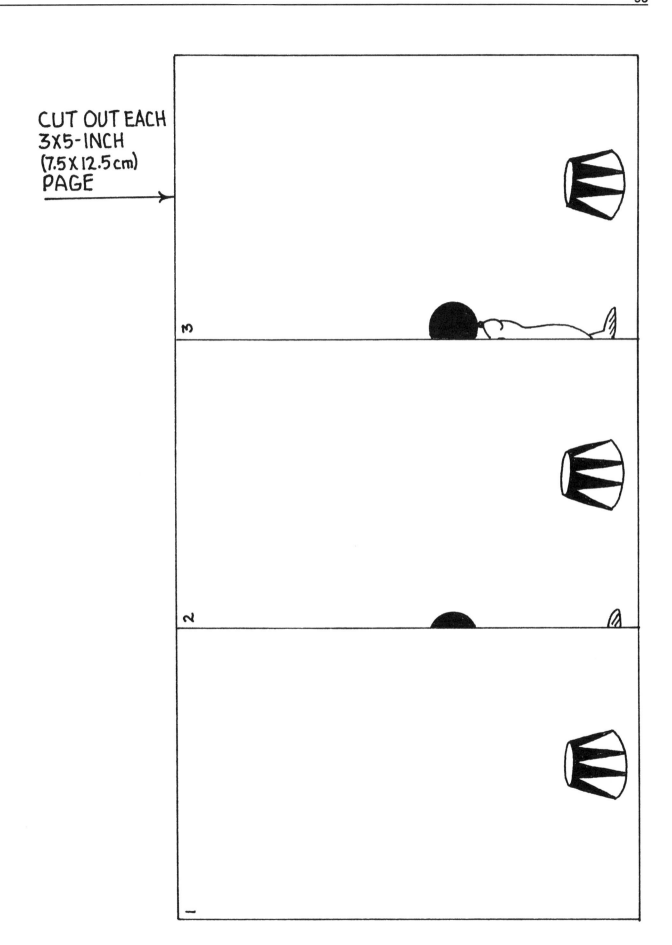

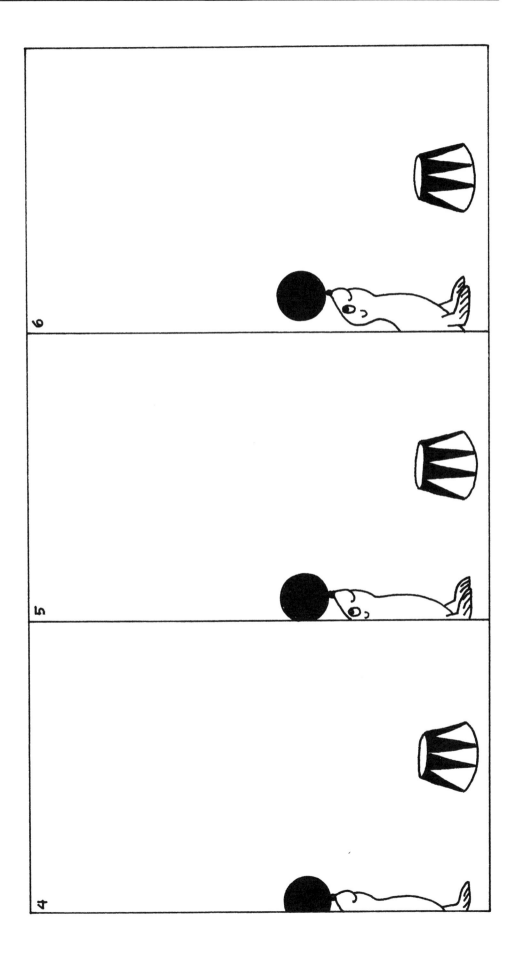

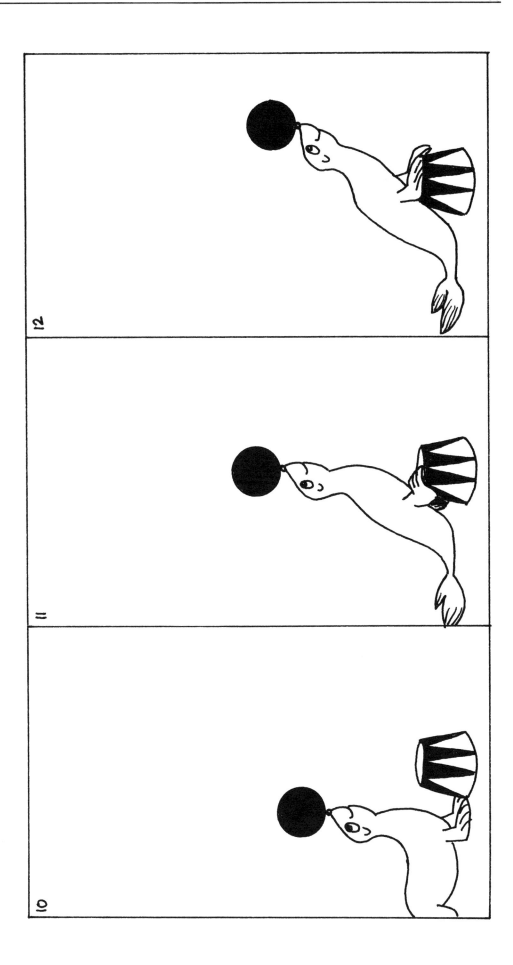

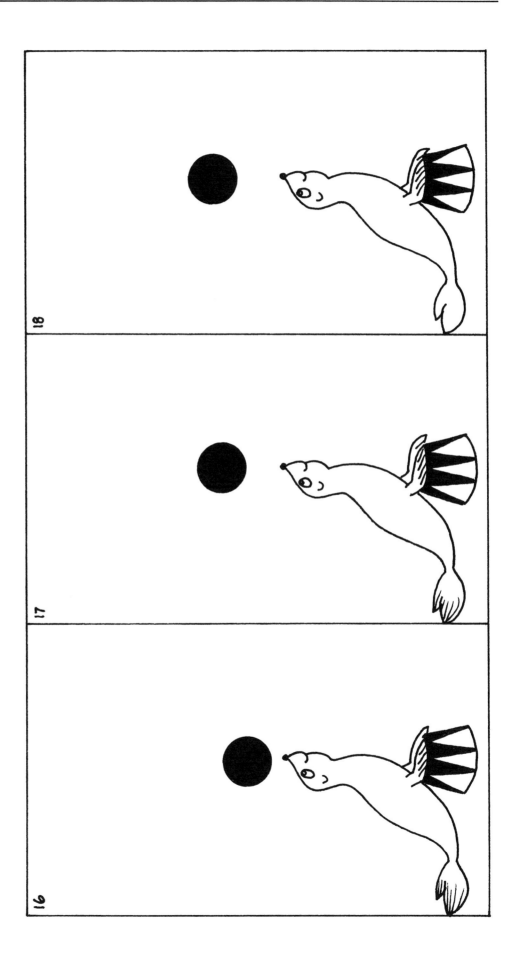

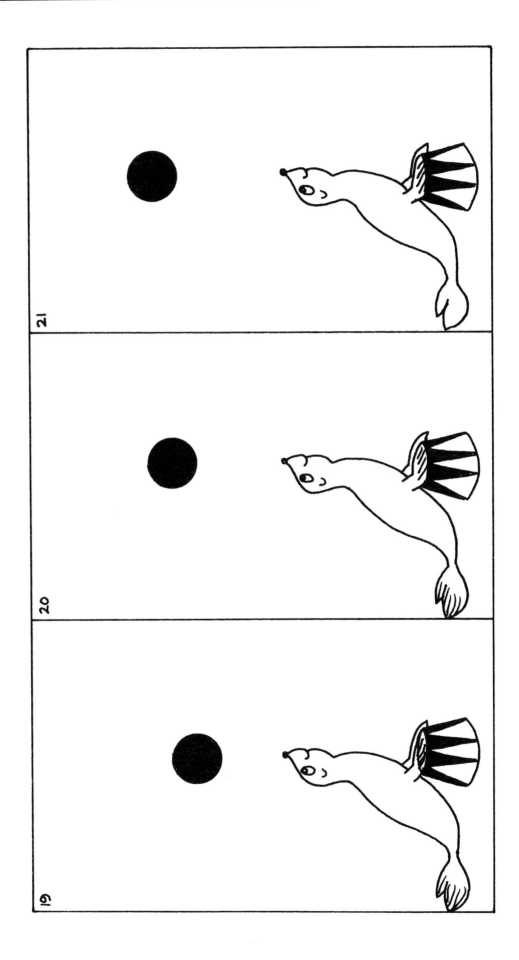

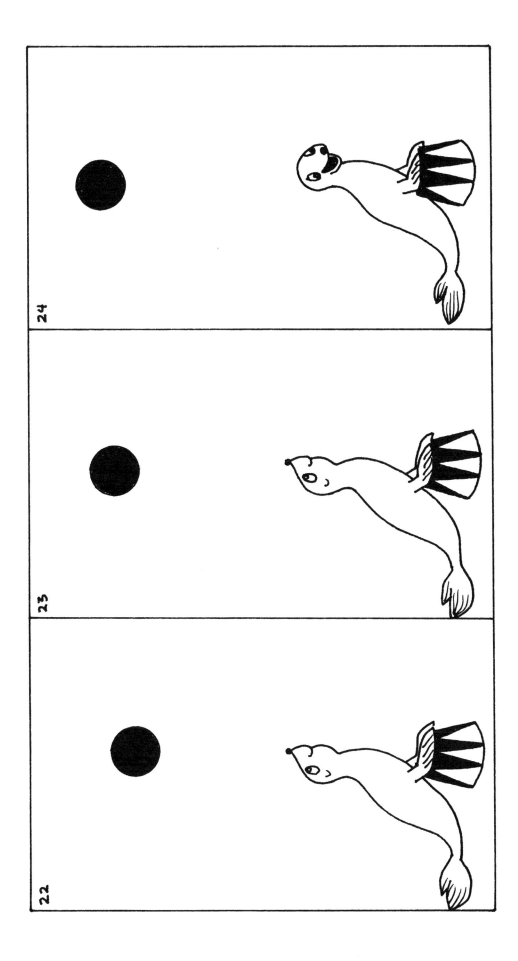

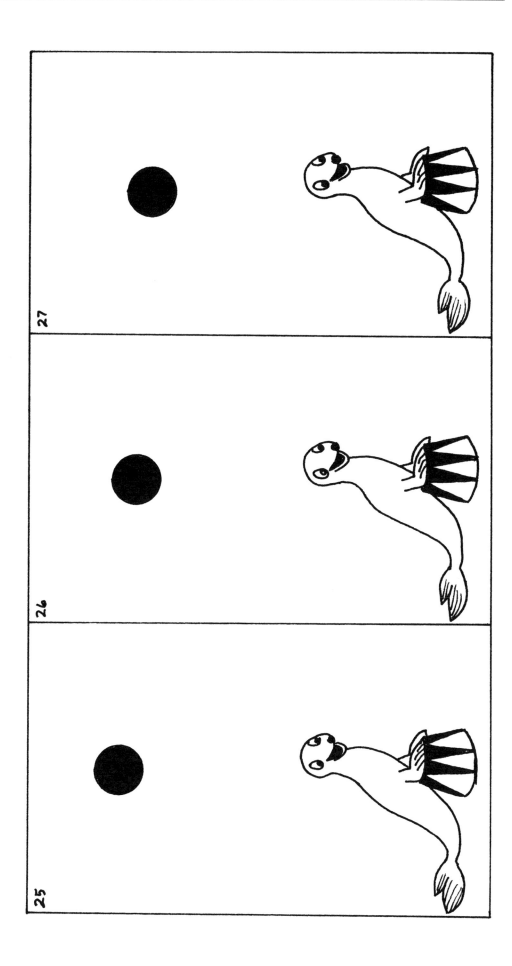

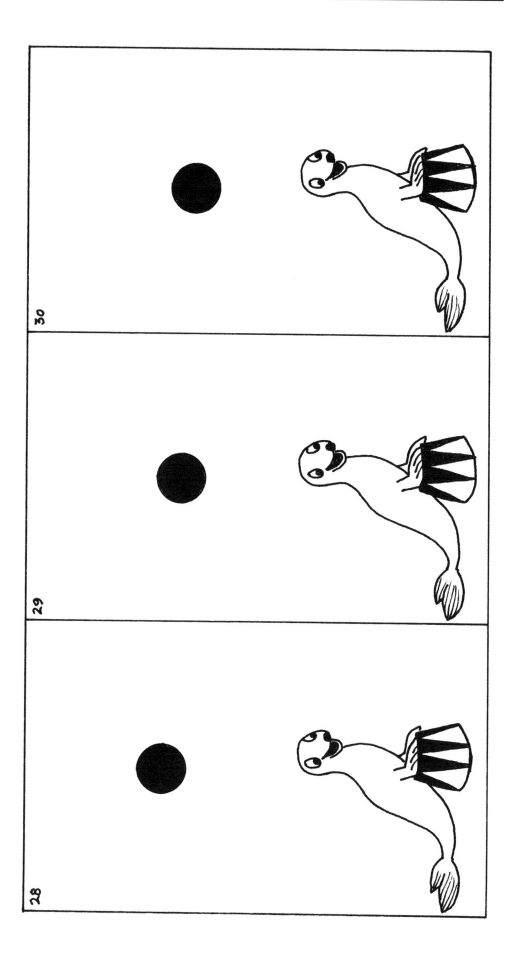

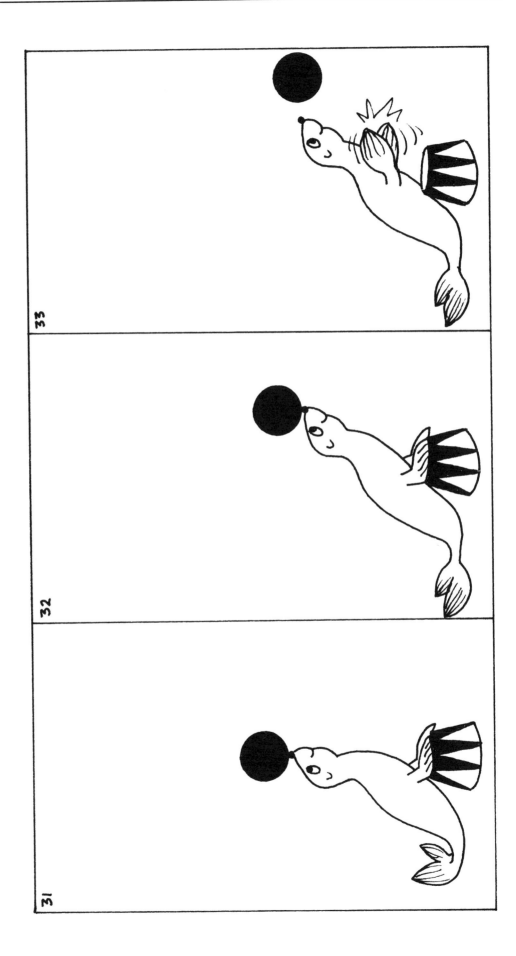

DIRECTIONS ON PAGE 25 SHOW HOW TO BIND YOUR FLIP BOOK TOGETHER.

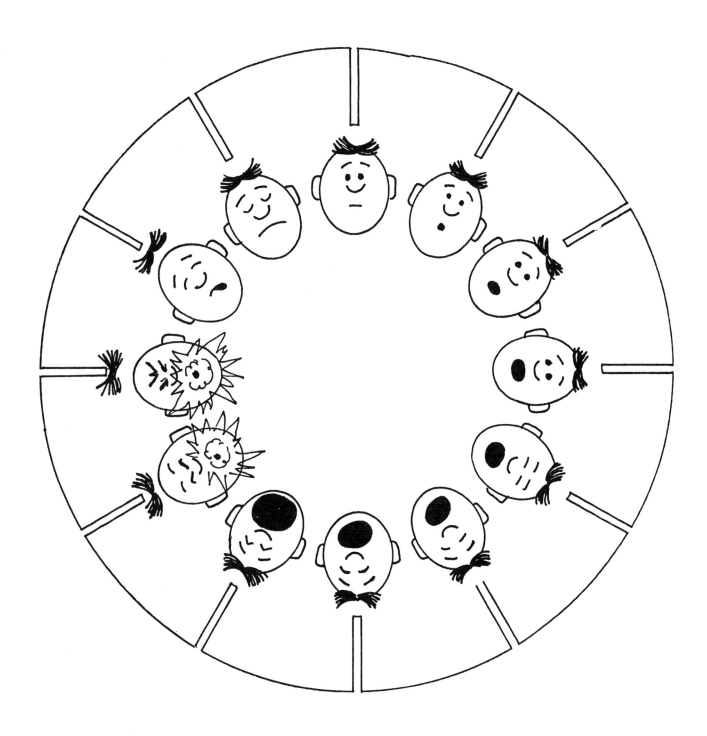

PHOTOCOPY THE SNEEZER ABOVE AND GLUE TO A CARDBOARD DISC.

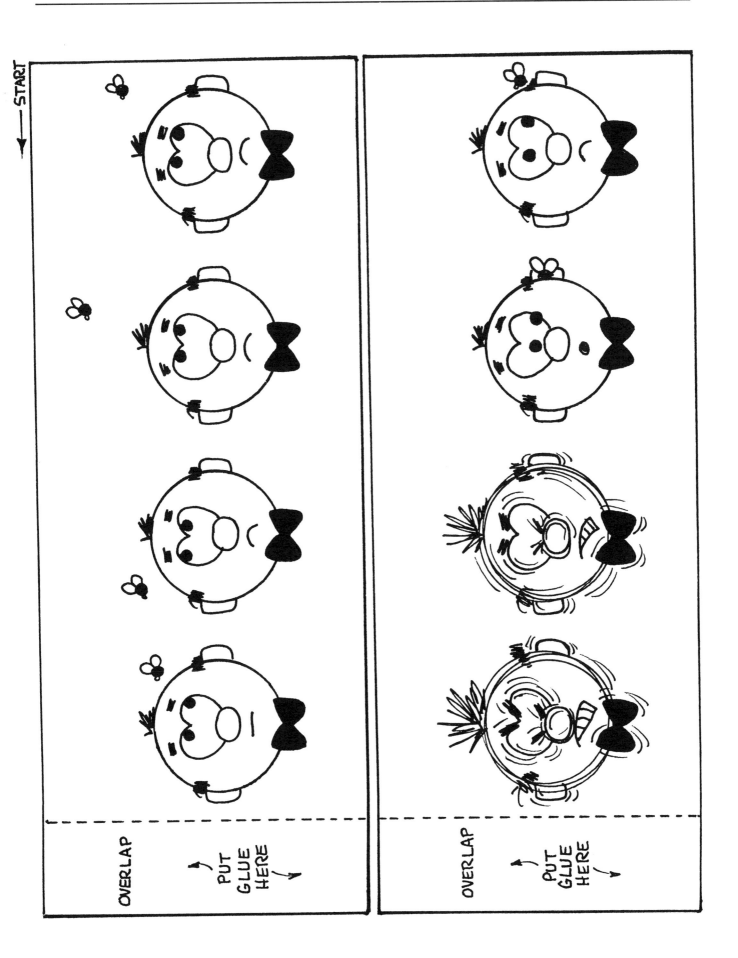

Trace or photocopy the three sections, then cut out and glue them together. Use the same dimensions when drawing your own zoetrope strips.

Index

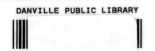